MIGRATIONS

ALSO BY PHYLLIS BECK KATZ

All Roads Go Where They Will (poetry)

MIGRATIONS

Poems by

Phyllis Beck Katz

*For Louise,
and for her
own migrations.
with best wishes*

[signature]

Antrim House

Simsbury, Connecticut

Library of Congress Control Number: 2013949428

ISBN: 978-1-936482-56-6

Printed & bound by United Graphics, Inc.

Book design by Rennie McQuilkin

Front cover photograph by Arnold M. Katz

Author photograph by Ellen Augarten

Antrim House
860.217.0023
AntrimHouse@comcast.net
www.AntrimHouseBooks.com
21 Goodrich Road, Simsbury, CT 06070

For my children Paul, Sarah, Amy and Laura,
best perennials of all my gardens

ACKNOWLEDGEMENTS

The following publications and displays issued earlier versions of poems appearing in this volume:

Birchsong: Poetry Centered in Vermont: "Pumpkins on the River," "Union Village Dam, Spring Flood 2011"

Bloodroot Literary Magazine: "Going Through: Reflections on a Postcard with a Photograph of Paulette and André," "Ode to Her Yellow Bathing Suit," "On Climbing Ayers Rock," "Tears," "Wings"

The Mountain Troubador: "Out of Fire"

Poem City's Poetry Month Displays 2011, 2012, 2013: "An Irruption of Pine Siskins," "Morning," "Rehearsal of Bach's Cantata 119"

I gratefully acknowledge a continuing debt to the encouragement and support of the Still Puddle Poetry Group (founded in 1995 and still meeting each month); to my Provincetown poetry friends, especially to Wendy Drexler for her fine-tuned editing of some of my poems. In addition, my thanks to Christopher Bursk for his generosity in reading and editing the first version of this manuscript, and to Wyn Cooper for his thoughtful and critical editing of second and third versions. My thanks also for inspiring and generative workshops at The Frost Place with Martha Rhodes, Christopher Bursk, and Daniel Tobin; at the Fine Arts Work Center with Vijay Seshadri, Marie Howe, Nick Flynn, and Alan Shapiro; and for several workshops in Norwich, Vermont with a group of fellow poets under the mentorship of Cynthia Huntington. Finally, my deepest gratitude for his skilled work on this book to Rennie McQuilkin, outstanding editor, publisher, and poet.

TABLE OF CONTENTS

Sometimes Pangloss told Candide: "All things that occur are connected in the best of all possible worlds; for in the end if you had not been driven from a beautiful castle with a great kick on your rear end because of your love for Miss Cunégonde, if you had not been thrust into the inquisition, if you had not traveled America on foot, if you had not struck the baron with a good blow of your sword, or lost all your sheep from the fine land of Eldorado, you would not be eating preserved citron and pistachios here." "That is well said," answered Candide, "but we must cultivate our garden."

Voltaire, *Candide*, Chapter XXX
Translation by Phyllis Beck Katz

I.

Wrestling with Angels

They come at night, my angels,
wings beating, drumming me hollow,
summoning me to war. Their wings
rack me, open me to who I am, who I am not.
No blessings come with them like Jacob's,
no promises of glory for me or my kin.

At dawn I wake, sheets wrinkled, drenched,
mind bruised, bloodied, angel gone. To ignore
the echo of my angel's beating drum, I rise
and go outside to tend my garden, turn
those seeds of torment hard under the earth.

To Plant My Garden

I am a shadow in a dark box.
It is cold. I am locked in.
No key. No way out.

My mind will not bend.
In the box, my body
pretends to sleep.

Words, phrases,
whose shapes
I thought I knew

dissolve in a river
full of sorrow. I am alone
in the mud, the dark

till moonlight forms
a path. I must reach it
to plant my garden.

No one is one.
I must find the key
to open the box,

to become a woman who
will cultivate her garden
till her world ends.

Night Scream

It came from the woods,
past midnight, our house
asleep. A cry shattered
the silence, anguished,
a keening yelp, a howl,
perhaps a rabbit, captured
in the brush by a hunting owl,
its agony piercing the open
window, an arrow shooting
through my ear drums to lodge
its razor-sharp point in my heart.

How could I return to sleep,
with this sound of death
ringing in the room, how could I,
hearing that night scream, fail
to know it might have been mine?

On Climbing Ayers Rock

It is not the great red sandstone rock itself
that terrifies, though the way it rises, an island
in the dry and barren plain impresses,
not its height or girth, nor its isolation,
not its age or geological origin.

No. But there's a power in the rock
you do not feel when you begin. You think
it's just a rock, a giant sandstone,
another climb you want to make and will.

It's not the warning signs you've read below,
lists of those who've fallen to their deaths –
you've climbed before, have stood on canyon rims,
walked paths too narrow for a mountain goat.
You know the risks. You've never fallen.
You think it's just an ordinary climb.

It's not. It is not the going up the naked trail,
the hand rope you must stoop to reach,
or the way the bending slope offers no place
to catch you if you slip,
but half way up, you sense a force
that wants you down.

You've read the sign
that tells you the aborigines
will not climb this rock
but hold it sacred, its trail a dream track
only spirits walk. For them
the great rock's name is Uluru.

It's not that you're a coward, not
that you believe in spirits. You don't.
But you have felt a sudden earthquake
in your heart, a trembling weakness in your legs,
and a hand that wants to push you off.

Tattoos: Cold December Night on a Packed "A" Train

In front of me, in my face, it's so close,
a naked arm, covered with black-inked tattoos.
Its owner, in thread-bare trousers and white t-shirt,
left arm covered by his jacket, right arm naked,
on full display, catalogues his trophy arm
for anyone who asks: down from his shoulder,
his biceps, to his wrist, and all around, inked
images of New York landmarks: the Chrysler Building,
Grand Central Station, the Twin Towers, still standing,
Empire State Building, Statue of Liberty, and more.
His New York arm, he confesses just before his stop,
took one full day on each of ten weeks. The value
of his tattooed arm, he boasts, outweighs its costs
in money, time, and pain.

We rattle on uptown, and I reflect on how many times
we've moved – enough for a full body of tattoos:
 D.C., Boston, London, L.A., Tenafly, Chicago, Sparkill,
Heidelberg, Farmington, and now, Norwich, Vermont.
Each place has left incisions etched indelibly
beneath, not on, my aging skin.

Out of Fire, 1961

Hot winds are blowing down from the high desert –
this year's Santa Ana.
I am waiting for our first child –
the relentless hot days and torrid nights
press hard on my swollen belly. The child
will not come, the winds will not stop
burning the air, drying the nearby hills.

The fire starts on a dry slope, and spreads.
We leave our stifling apartment,
go to a high roof-top to witness
the canyons burn, the trees explode
like rockets, first one house and then
another erupting in flame. We watch
the inferno hurdle from hilltop to hilltop
in a night sky red with fire and black
with soot and smoke. We see birds fly up
and out beyond the blazing hills.

Days later the child inside me kicks
at the walls that hold him in. The fire
has flickered down to smoldering ruins,
the canyons blackened, bereft of life.
The sharp ember within me kindles,
quickens, swells, grows, and rages
until I am consumed by the burning
that grips tighter and tighter inside me –
I become all heat, all fire, and our son bursts free.

Nestlings

Red-winged blackbirds screaming around him,
I have watched the hungry red-tailed hawk
perched up at the yew's tip, blackbirds winging closer,
hawk curling its talons fast on the branch.
I have felt the fear of the fleeing orioles and sparrows,
the desperation of the blackbirds battling for their young,
and have seen the striking of the hawk's breast
by the boldest blackbird, the startled wingspread jump
of the hawk, his return again to his hunter's perch,
sharp golden beak glinting in the sun,
above a placid ocean that licks the shore,
near the mudflats where tiny crabs scuttle,
yellow-lined claws tucked on their backs, their young
in deep nest holes safe from prying beaks.
I have heard the tide beginning to rise again,
seen the hawk still perched on the tree, still waiting,
whirlwind of blackbirds down-diving around him,
a toddler running off on the path below,
his parents following to catch and hold him fast.

Daily Pages at the Cancer Center

Each fortressed by a skin of personal pain,
our ears closed to the cries in the corridor,
inarticulate howls that rise and grow
outside the waiting room – avoiding the sight
of the bald woman with eye sockets that lie
on separate planes, emaciated mouth twisted,
who moves slowly towards the screeching,
we read our newspapers, check our email,
shut our eyes when the boy in the wheel chair
arrives, whose protests escalate in pitch
despite his father's trying to calm him down,
or when the older boy beside them,
who drags one leg beside his dangling arm
trips and begins to cry, or when the mother
reaches the three, her family, cannot help,
and turns back to her seat in tears –
cocooning ourselves as if their suffering
were happening in another world
that most of us, while feeling, will ignore –
a body burning in a square, a dead child
wrapped in a bloody blanket, images
that reach us only through the distance
of daily pages we can quickly turn.

Tears

after Carol Duffy

There are some days when I can't cry.
Some days the tears flow in torrents,
a flood that washes me awake.

There are tears in the pages of the books I have read,
tears for places I can name, but have never seen:
Bangladesh, Biafra, Aleppo, Darfur.

Who knows what can hold all these tears?
When I try to catch them, they change to stars,
and I see them falling.

Breakage

I dreamt that the angel who breaks
up marriages attacked a house I loved,
on a dead, wet day when summer's warmth
had vanished and someone had walked
away and left an empty place at the table.
I dreamt of the house waiting for
the final separation, ripping away
of its foundations, days of growth
and building torn in shreds, images
of the future black with absence,
the rupturing of all – plaster dropping
from the ceiling, paint flaking off walls,
floors cracking open, doors and windows
slashed in shards of wood and glass,
the only sounds the dripping of
a rusty faucet, ticking of a forgotten clock.

An Irruption of Pine Siskins

A trembling of tiny finches
ravaged a thistle sock last week,
emptying its contents every day.
Arriving as a group
they fed communally,
each striving for a perfect perch,
their rapid back and forth
from branch to feeder
a recapitulation in a fugue of motion,
its theme and counterpoint
developed in their frantic need
for food, their fear of predators.
Now they have left
as suddenly as they appeared,
their agitated flight
a constant tremulo
that speaks of dangers
coming on the wind.

On Seeing a Plaster Cast
of a Dog in Pompeii

Now he lies on his back,
legs stretched up, mouth
gasping for his final breath,
killed in an instant
by a pyroclastic surge,
frozen and decomposing
for centuries in hardened ash
until only his hollow shape
remained for Fiorelli to cast
in poured plaster.

Chained to the threshold
when the lava came, he was left
to guard an empty house
as the others fled.
But that morning, I like to think,
he trotted out the door
down the polished stones
of the narrow street to find
a butcher's bone, a crust
the baker threw into the alley
or a wedge of cheese whose mold
could be ignored, that he moved freely
with the purpose of any dog going about
the usual business of his life,
and did not know he had fetched his last
stick, had barked for the last time
at the stranger at his door.

The Universe Without the Higgs Boson

Like moonlight, we would
be weightless unless this particle

gave us mass and substance.
Without the Boson, our lives

would be only *so much gardening
in the dark.* We would be trapped

at the edge of a fallow field
where a rusted plow marks

the last furrow. Underground
we would listen to earthworms,

voiceless in the mole's tunnel
without that moment

when the law of balance tips,
and our gardens grow.

*Everything interesting,
including ourselves*

*results from flaws or breaks
in the symmetry –*

without these gaps we are
bodiless shades

formless without the dropped
stitch in the knitted row.

II.

Morning

First light. A few cars rumble
past, a solitary jay complains
from the tall pine, a muffled runner
moves thin determined legs
along the dark road. The air feels
cold and empty, with nothing
to show that I was here, whirl
of the wind's passing. The fox
leaves his scent on the tree roots
for the world to smell, while I
have made few tracks in the earth's
mud, left none of my hair caught
in the barbed wire around the pasture
from a daring leap for the freshness
of spring buds, my voice drowned
by chattering finches in the bare birch.

Wings

In the rain, I went to the river,
mind full of stones of despair.
I was cold and wet, heart full of dread.

That morning I saw a Bald Eagle
dive three times down into the river
after a muskrat, rise three times,
come up claws empty. No quitter,
he dove again, hooked talons
folded tight to his captive's back,

and with his wings he swam the river,
rowing the water's smooth surface
and brought his catch ashore.
I needed wings.

Way of the River

When there are no dreams,
sleep is dark as the river
that flows beyond my house, mind

and body yielding to its steady glide
as if I were floating from the source to the mouth
and would go on to cross wide seas that never

reach land, a passage with no coming back, a sleep
I cannot summon or refuse, a sleep
where desire does not dwell, where pain is gone.

When dreams come, my mind pretends to sleep,
and my body opens to strange places
where seeds I thought I'd sowed with care

sprout odd and unfamiliar plants: sorghum
and sassafras for snowdrops, or poison oak
where peonies should have grown, a baby goat

in the nursery crib, a flight to Barcelona
landing on Saturn, an avalanche of snow
on a mountain in Oodanatta, a heat-wave

at Vostok Station. When these dreams come
and I awake, I don my waders, take my buckets,
and go to the river. I wash my dreams away.

The Great Wave Near Kanagata:
One of Hokusai's Thirty-Six Prints of Mount Fuji

In these paintings, disaster never happens.
No fire, no lava explodes from the volcano's mouth –
a wave rises, looms, crests, but never breaks.
Here a snow-capped volcano floats beyond the *oikinami,*
that huge wave about to break over *oshiokuri-buno,*
fragile boats hurrying to port with passengers and catch.
Above the tiny crafts, the sky glows pink and white,
the wave's delicate drops of foam a benediction,
not a curse, the far distant mountain, an indifferent
observer. For Hokusai, artist of the *ukiyo-e,*
evanescent moment, the wave is poised where beauty
and disaster exist in a precarious equilibrium.
Here life stands in balance, moment just before
the wave breaks, the bomb falls, tornado rips.
I keep a copy of his picture to remind me.

Union Village Dam, Spring Flood 2011

I walk towards the silence that calls me
from the noises of this world: blaring music,
sirens, beeps of horns, voices using words
or telling stories I do not want to hear.
I climb up past the last house beyond the turning
where the roiling water born of this year's great spring rains
tumbles through the tunnel and flows roaring out
beneath the dam swelling the river banks as it goes.
I stand on the giant edifice of stones and concrete
built so many years ago to hold back the floods
that once devoured the towns below its slope
and see a spreading lake, where before the waters
rose so high, there were near-dry rivulets
meandering slowly through stagnant mud,
matted cat-tails, clotted clumps of honeysuckle,
and sand banks tracked by sandpipers and sparrows,
where now still water widens over trees and trails,
haven for rafts of ducks resting from long flights,
for silhouettes of hawks and ravens gliding
across the clear surface, for logs floating free.
I look down into the water's depths and see
another world untouched by life's loud intrusions,
and though the lake will slowly sink, the dirt roads
and trails, song birds nesting in the brush, return,
I do not want this earth to dry again. I want
to hold this silence born of water, to dive
into this deeper world – and stay.

Pumpkins on the River

When the clouds burst
and torrents of rain fell
after days and days of drought,
the dry earth opened wide
its parched lips to drink,
and the river filled with
gladness, swelling above
its thirsty banks and
flooding a wide field
full of ripened pumpkins.
One by one the pumpkins,
wrested from their stalks
by the rising water,
floated away
from their roots
and left the soil
where they had grown.
You could see lines
of liberated pumpkins
stretching for miles,
moving to the river's
pull. For them, no rude
cutting of their flesh
into faces they did not
know, no wrenching out
of guts and seeds,
no candle scorching
their hollowed bellies,
no boiling, baking, stewing,
roasting. Free, they sailed

on unharmed, nodding gently
to the moving current,
as if consenting to its will,
and as they passed,
I longed to join them,
to leave the vines that bind me,
to follow as they journeyed
down river to the sea.

Where the Garden Was, Stones

When the wild horses came thundering through
meadows my heart was bare, an open flower,
but now I am vanishing into the fog of a sullen day.
And everywhere is darkness and barren earth;
above me cycles a whirlwind; I cannot tend the garden.

Catching Zhuangzi

Two dozen swallowtail butterflies
once feasted on the cone flowers
outside my kitchen door,

saffron wings among
the purple blossoms. I have never
dreamt of butterflies, though

I have read that to dream of them
tells us we are imagining
our own transformation

at the end of a cycle
of growth and change, wings
opening, flying free. I would like

to fly, but I do not have the vision
of Zhuangzi, who asleep
dreamt he was a butterfly,

and when he woke, he did not know
if he was himself again
or a butterfly

dreaming he was a man.
Today I dreamt I caught
Zhuangzi in my net

and let him go.

III.

Lost Memories

I tried to remember my ancestors,
called up their names and places,
summoned them to speak.
They came as shades, and faded
back into their darkness before
I heard their stories. I tried to catch them
in my arms, but could not hold them –
the sagas of my past were lost, my parents
burying their beginnings beneath their lives
together, both offering now and then
at most a fleeting image from a past
they did not want to share.

I found a book of memories beneath
my pillow, leaves tattered, pages of the past –
old family lore, mixed with stories that are mine.
I tried to salvage what I could.

My Great Aunt

1. Her Diary

On an attic shelf an old felt hat
slumps beside a battered box

in which a diary,
inked letters broken,

lies closed. She wore
the hat until the feather

molted, filled the diary
then left it on that shelf

abandoned. In it – her life –
no going forward,

no turning back,
stuck in a spinster's world

that she would never leave.
She wrote it all and

let it rot alone, unread,
hat and diary aging together

on that attic shelf,
below them

the leather trunk in which she hid
keepsakes that said what she could not.

2. The Things She Kept

In the trunk, her photo. Her eyes do not smile,
as the steamer carries her across weeks
and miles of empty sea to Shanghai. It is 1913.

She stayed four years, filled thin journals –
dates of music lessons, tea parties, birthdays.
Inside that trunk, the things she kept:

(1) four small white-faced Chinese dolls
in satin smocks for use in spells,
round black skull caps above their pigtails;

2) a miniature stone coffin –
within, an ivory corpse, shrouded
to keep against a coming death;

3) two exquisite pairs of tiny slippers,
made for young girls to offer the goddess
who eases the pain of bound and broken feet;

(4) sheets that she'd crocheted, sealed in folds
of faded tissue, trousseau she would never use,
and written in fine cursive script, a simple note:

"Sewn in 1911 for my wedding to —"
the name crossed out.

Lotus Shoes

When the girl was six
her mother gave her
a pair of tiny shoes
to offer to the goddess
who cared for women's ills,
lotus flowers floating
on their satin pink brocade –

goddess who turned
her face away
when the pain began,
toes bent
until they broke,
bones crushed.

Two times summer came
and went and autumn blew
to winter's frozen streams,
winter melted
into buds of spring,
before her feet were healed
enough to bear her
without pain.

When she was twelve
she was betrothed
and married to a man,
owner of a nearby farm,
rich man who desired
her for her tiny feet,
feet he never saw

in little shoes that covered
bent and twisted bones.

When she became a mother
she sewed new pairs
of tiny lotus shoes
for her infant daughters
for them to give the goddess
when their feet were bound.

A Conversation

after Horace, Odes I. 23

Horace:

Why does the fawn
shun the movement
in the field
and think it threatens her?

Why does she avoid
her ripeness and
deny that she
has reached the
season for a mate?

Chloe:

How does a young girl
come to guess
what all men want
before she's ready
to let them have it?

How does she feel
the power
of her sex
before she knows
it's there?

Why does she want
her body to mature
yet fears and hates
its ripening?

Why is she angry
at her need
to be protected,
confused by her
desire to taste the world?

Pink Champagne

She came to the big city to grow up,
found a rooming house she could afford,
was on her way.

She made no friends in the rooming house,
was afraid to leave her room, visited the common
bathroom, the shower, even the kitchen,
when the other roomers were out or were asleep.
Then she met someone.

She was tempted by his offer of champagne,
intrigued by his allure, so charming, so polite.
and so she took the glass he gave her,
loved the taste, the prickling of the bubbles
down her throat, liked how warm, how loose,
how attractive she began to feel, but when he tried
to caress her, she drained her glass, and bolted.

She took another room in another rooming house,
longed for more champagne, yearned to meet
another man, wanted to touch him and be touched,
to feel his arms around her, to be kissed, and maybe
more, desired it all, but wasn't sure she should .

Her Yellow Bathing Suit

Once you were satin-sleek.
Petite, constructed of three triangles
and braided cord, you had a price tag
worthy of your designer name.

You gleamed canary bright, crackled
electrical with filaments,
and if you'd had a voice, it would have said
"My singing is unique."

Displayed in the central window
of a shop along a boulevard in Nice,
you were enchanting. Soon you were wrapped
in sequined tissue, purchased

to enhance the well-oiled body
of a butter-stick brunette.
She never got you wet, but you were
never made for swimming.

your perfection lay in your allure.
You loved the way you hugged her breasts
and settled low upon her hips.
Once you felt adored, inspired lust,

Now you lie in tatters
at the bottom of a back street barrel
with others of your kind,
all out of style .

May you not be forgotten,
your splendor survive forever
in my song.

Going Through: Reflections on a Postcard with a Photograph of Paulette and André

The two children have lived through a war.
They sit posed facing each other
on a stone bench in a small French town.
It is 1949.

The children's war was across the ocean.
We were not hurt by their war.
Our wars happened at home.

In the picture the children are smiling
shyly at each other.

Our parents used to
pose my brother and me;
we sat where we were told.
In our pictures, we had to smile
for our father and for our mother.

The two children's elbows touch.
Their knees bend towards each other,
hands awkward on their laps.

We did not touch in our father's photos.
He never sat us close together. We did not
know what to do with our hands.

The girl in the photo has a big white bow
in her hair; the boy's is neatly combed and short.

Our mother had beautiful dark curly hair
and sad, frightened eyes.
I have her hair,

but it is not dark. Our mother was a dancer
who had to give up the dance.

The children's father may have fought
in the war.

Our father did not fight in the war.
He fought with himself.
He conquered our mother, battled us.
He never swallowed his anger.
He could not keep it down.

Beyond the children a wide dark door yawns open,
and a shadowed man watches.
The children do not see that he is watching.

Our father's anger watched us.
We felt his eyes on us,
his eyes on our mother.

One day the children in the photo
will have to go through the door,
wherever it leads.

Every house has a dark door
behind a wall. What you can see
in a picture is not what is there
behind the wall. We cling to our moments
of happiness when we can. Then we go through.

Dancer's Dream

for my mother

When you untied your toe shoes
and put away your tutu,
your ballroom gowns,
it was for good
although you did not know it.

You thought you could dance
a dance of love with him
in two-step or in waltz
and that your pas de deux
or tango would never end –

you thought he'd raise
his steady arms, hold you
tight, and dance with you
across the coming years,
and never
ever
let you
fall.

Brief Harmony

Each molded by life's varied clays –
a sibling lost, a child, our parents gone,
our times together shrinking as we'd aged,
I had not thought a visit with my brother
would bring our childhood closeness back,
for lately we seldom chose to speak about the past –
our own worlds full of present joys and sorrows,
both of us agreeing there was nothing left to say,
and we could not talk of politics or God,
but when he asked if I recalled the songs
our father sang to us, when after dinner
we washed up together, I could sing them all
with him, those songs of war and loss,
of fear and love, belief and doubt:

Pack up Your Troubles in your Old Kit Bag,
Just Say Goodbye to Mother,
There's Potatoes in the Oven,
Swing Low, Sweet Chariot,
and the poor maid Belle,
who lit the stove with dynamite,
but must be up in heaven –
she was too green to burn.

Our songs united us that rainy day
as once they had before, our harmony
evoking those harsh wars within our house
that song erased, reminding us how leaving home

had brought us pleasure more than pain,
but also bringing back the smells
of dinner, the laughter in the kitchen
when our father left his cares behind –

and then, our singing over,
the moment came unspun.

Choir Boy

for my father

I think your singing sprang from deep within,
where childhood innocence still had a home,
place you must have fortressed long ago
while still a boy although your high clear voice
could sometimes pierce those walls that closed you in,
moments when the tightness in your throat released.

I thought of how you let your rage and brooding
go, time when most of what you were was lost
for good and what remained was tuneless
and remote. You had become a frightened ghost
who saw his own reflection in a mirror
and fled from it in terror, a man who locked
his door against intruders only he could see.
No sudden brightness in your vacant face,
no whispered echo of the boy who once
could sing as if he were an angel – nothing
but your empty shell.

Parenting

It was like the favorite dress I'd kept so long.
Years after our marriage, our children grown,
I kept trying it on again, tugging it over my hips,
unwilling to admit the fit was off for good.
I dreamed of my old home, seduced by memories –
gnarled apple tree by a window full of blossoms,
songs in the kitchen, twilight stickball in the street,
cowbell ringing to call us in, milk and stories
before sleep. For years, these pictures of the past
sufficed to swallow up my childhood's darker days –
my father's rages, my mother's martyrdom and silence.

But when my parents, unprepared for growing old,
no longer hid behind the curtains of their need, clutter
of magazines, piles of laundry, and unpaid bills,
I parented my parents. I cleaned and cooked and comforted,
until their breathing slowed and ceased, and they were gone,
and afterwards, I swore our children's coming home
would never end like mine. And now, they all are grown,
still coming home, to find us aging – balance slowly tipping.

Till the Wind Changes

Breakfast: whispers of coffee, toast, the sizzling
of bacon. They are waiting for their grandson
to join them, waiting and waiting. They hear
a thunderclap of feet, a north wind,

no, a tornado booming above them,
and a swirling wind tunnel
of muzzled anger, sullen clouds,
a miasma darkening the room.

They say, "Good morning."
He, now as lifeless as the Salton Sea,
uncombed hair hanging
over eyes and ears,

sags into a chair, shoulders
bunched, back rounded against
their voices, a glacial icepack
they cannot melt, grunts something

that sounds like "uh." And though his body
sits there among them, the boy flies
out the window, across the driveway
above the roof and up and up to reach

his own planet, his own galaxy,
inhabited by his own people,
leaving them behind,
waiting for the wind to change
the way it would.

IV.

Chickadees

The brighter longer February days
do all the work; silent birds
sing out again their high pealed song,
in light that trumps the coldest day,
song that wakes our winter sleep and changes all.
The woods, so quiet under winter's rule,
now open to the music of desire,
a song of songs that echoes through the trees,
in pairs of notes of balanced intervals,
repeated sweet refrain. It is that brightening
of the sky, driving of darker days away,
that tells the birds to sing –
their urgent voices pierce the winter woods:
choose me, choose me.

Wings Beating Inside Her

he said he knew her answer
but he had asked no question
his voice looked beyond a wilderness
of deserts unexplored
she hot and dry and waiting

he asked her if she would
and the grasses in the meadow
were bent by a touch so soft
she could not breathe
to feel

Song of the Leopard Seal
in Paradise Bay

In Antarctica's summer waters
we found a giant Leopard Seal,
sunning on an solitary ice floe.
Eyes closed as if asleep,
the seal began to sing
in bubbled notes
that rose and fell in spirals,
a punctuated pulse
of hollowed *o's* and *a's*
and rounded *e's* and *u's,*
music that spoke of
longing and desire.
And we remembered.

The Real Game

When the cloud of feathers floated by,
a steady stream of downy white and gray,
past the lilac bush bereft of leaves,
past the maple tree with its crooked trunk,
I watched them from the window
in the hall beyond our bedroom
where, last night, we had argued
with rare ferocity till you exploded and
I cried, and then we went to sleep.

Feathers flew through the air, like leaves
sailing free before snow. I saw them
pirouette and glide, dancers warming up
in morning chill, and traced them to their
source. Crouched on a slender branch,
a Northern Shrike was butchering a chickadee
he'd impaled there, plucking off the feathers
as he ate, his savagery beggaring our dispute,
his brutality a necessity for him, our arguments
a game we do not play for keeps.

Suggestions for a Long Marriage

Let's break through the block that separates
us, closed space where we can't breathe,
place where knots on knots tie us apart –
square, hitch, bow, splice. Let's refresh
the stagnant air, allow a breeze
to sing its songs, defeat that loss of hearing
choking us with words we cannot swallow.
Let's overthrow custom, habit, old ways
of what, dare I say it, feels too long a marriage,
where it's too easy to ricochet sideways
downhill into irritations, refutations.

As our years accumulate, our time
to share them growing shorter, threatening
to disappear for good, let's find again
the voices we once knew, still present
but so difficult to hear, let's let them roar,
drown out the silence that deafens us,
shout out in words and music only we can hear.

V.

Angel of the Future

One black night, an angel of death
came to sit on my pillow.
It raised black wings above
me, breathed noxious fumes around
me, stretched long bony fingers
towards my neck and hissed into my ear
that it was time, but I said, "No, not now,"
and wrestled until the angel fled.
Cold and weak, I woke at last
from my long battle, hair streaked
with gray, fingers bent and knotted,
skin dry and wrinkled, and I knew the angel
would come again.

Weather Report

Between flashes of lighting
shaking our roof, claps of forked bolts
rattling windows or shutters,
thunder booming out of great mountains
of black-building clouds, between raging winds
that plough the air, breaking tree
limbs and trunks, felling the old,
bending the weak, between whirlwinds
of leaves dropping onto mud-puddled earth
wild streams ripping away bridges,
houses, trees, stones, roads as they go –

between all devastating gales
outside that come as they will,
and the storm in our house
brewing in your cells where cancer
has struck you again

there is no difference.

Rehearsal of Bach's Cantata 119

That day when the conductor abruptly put down her baton,
the music stopped in the middle of a bass aria,
gray-haired musicians frozen, still as statues,
bows raised, lips close to mouth-pieces, fingers poised
above piano keys, singers' scores open and held high.
We watched as the conductor approached the tenor
slumped in his chair, and gently touched his hand,
saw him lift his head trying to smile through lips bleached
white as the aureole of hair that crowned his head,
heard someone whisper *Call 911*, while another quickly rose to phone.

In silence, the players sat as the tenor's wife, so skilled
at coaxing arpeggios and trills from English horn and oboe,
spoke softly to her husband and packed her instruments,
her reeds and music and waited for the ambulance to arrive.
I could taste the fear in the room. Then, someone said
Let's play, and the conductor picked up her baton, the musicians
opened their music, and Bach's aria rose and fell in intricate
counterpoint – Jerusalem and its promise claimed us once again.

To Treetops, Sparkill, N.Y.

Have you forgotten us,
who gave you your first
face-lift, a fresh new look,
and showed you how your world

had changed? You had a shabby
elegance, lofty doors
and windows, dark green
shutters stately and forbidding,

proud Victorian matron,
hiding your crumbling foundation
with a skirt of violets and myrtle,
your slated mansard bonnet decked

with offerings from tulip trees
and oaks. Without us, would you
have seen your shabby servants'
quarters transformed to rain-

bowed rooms with swinging
beds and jungle-painted bath?
Without us would you have shed
the faded rose and ivy

on your walls, heard the notes
of trumpet or bassoon or flute,
seen the host of children
sledding on your sloping hill?

Without us, would you have lived
to notice, from the window
at your peak, smoke on the horizon
stretching to the south beyond

your sheltered fields and woods,
have watched the planes fly in and crash,
have seen the pair of shining towers
as they burned and fell?

Letter to Myself

Forget your fear your memory
is going, thought as crooked
as your arthritic fingers, difficult
to flex at will, aging molecules
in a brain unable to recall parts of your past.
Forget that this morning you could not
summon *Eggs Benedict* at breakfast
however much you tried.

Find comfort in involuntary triggers –
those luscious Proustian madeleines,
uninvited guests arriving in the empty
chambers of your mind: pungent smell
of horse sweat, softness of a baby's head,
taps at sunset, taste of mountain blueberries,
flute song of the Hermit Thrush, sudden
wind puffs ruffling a sleeping lake.

Last Year the Sky, 2011

Last year, the sky that swam above our house
was a dark dome, the land below it an inverted bowl,
bordered by hemlocks, birches, ash, and beech.
Once, years ago, we saw a dazzling display
of Northern Lights, steeples of green rising in jagged points
above the hills on the horizon, and one summer
we lay on blankets in our meadow for hours to watch
a Perseid shower fall across a dark star-spattered sky.

Our house was isolated; we could see only one light
in the hills beyond, could sometimes hear a car
on the dirt road below us, were protected from its headlights
by the forest around us. Sometimes a neighbor's dog
barked in the distance, sometimes a pack of coyotes howled
from the ridge opposite, and often the Barred Owl
called in the dark, or railed in loud dispute with an invader
owl as they negotiated whose woods these were.

We cherished those night sounds –
soft whispering trees, buzz of the cicadas,
urgent call of peepers in our pond in early spring.
We have seen the lightning, heard the thunder hammer
so close that we could feel its breath upon us.
Now we have left that place, those woods, the sky
we had each night, as full of darkness and of light
as the earth beneath it, as our lives. We will walk
new woods, dig new gardens while we can.

Migrations, 2012

Last spring a pair of tree swallows
came back to their summer home
in the meadow behind the school
that watches our new home, the birds
soaring together close over our heads,
skimming the field, blue-bird nest
boxes they would claim as theirs,
apple trees where they would perch,
watching for insects as the mist lifted,
shining blue-black backs gleaming
in the morning sun. They had come back
to mate, lay their eggs, raise their young,
and they swooped across the tall grass,
hard-wired for their yearly journey.
Not thinking of the warm sanctuary
they'd left behind, not longing for their
winter home, they'll come and go
each year, while we have left the house
we built together, its view across those miles
of woods and hills to the White Mountains,
its double rainbows overhead, its stars so bright
and close, our harbor from roar and rattle of trucks,
whine of motorcycles, exhaust of busses, loud voices
right outside our new door, strange dogs in our yard –
home to which we'll not return at summer's end,
place no longer refuge against our growing old.

Cold Coming, 2013

I know each corner of these new autumn woods
the turns and twists of every path, the roots,
sharp rocks that wait beneath the fallen oak
and maple leaves to trip me up once more.

I know the rock ledge where another Barred Owl
has its nest, the high pines now bereft of warblers,
the stone wall that once stood here all tumbled
down, but marking still the edges of a pasture

whose sheep devoured all the undergrowth.
I've seen the sun swallowed by the lurking hills,
the sickle moon climb up beyond the church,
glimpsed the white-tail deer as it ran,

traced the tracks of mink beside the muddy brook,
broken barbed wire on its bank, bits of rusted sheep fence.
Today, the meadow and the orchard were white
with hoar frost; I felt the chill of winter,

watched my young dog make circles in the grasses,
leap over piles of brush and stones in pure delight,
smelled the wood smoke from the house beyond
the orchard, listened to the swish of morning traffic,

rumble of the school bus, shouts of the children
in the playground before school, coats and shoes
and mittens cast off and left behind, remembered how
it was never to feel the cold, or count what years remained.

Mirror Image

after Denise Low

I see a younger woman of thirty dimly reflected
in my mirror tonight. She looks with weary eyes –
ready to fall into bed, into the sleep that comes
quickly after a day filled with teaching, child rearing,
cleaning, cooking –no time for it all. She does not think
beyond the next day. That is enough. I watch her close
her books, cover her children, turn off the light.
She has folded her wings. Her nest is safe.

When I look again, she has flown to the top of the old tulip tree,
on her way to cross new skies. She does not imagine beyond
her todays, cannot envision what I see in my glass.
She does not know her fledglings will fly far from the nest,
migratory journeys they will make, new places she will go,
switchbacks she will have to take. She does not imagine
that she will grow old.

Keeping Track

She hated the way words disappeared –
knew they were hiding somewhere

in her head. If only she could find them
the way she'd learned to look at mud and snow,

to tell if fox or coyote had left its trail,
a porcupine had waddled den to tree,

a fisher cat had bounded close behind it,
could recognize the mitten-shaped rear paws

of snow shoe hares, the marks the back feet made
before the front feet left their prints behind,

the nest the grouse would dig in snow drifts
to keep it safe. She'd gained the skills to read

those forest signs, but had no map to trace
for pieces missing from her store of words;

their shadows hid behind her tongue, refused
to speak. She blamed herself for losing names

of books, of movies she had seen, of plays,
forgetting an agreed on date to meet a friend.

Sometimes on winter days she saw the marks
of claws the bears made on the tree trunks

before their winter naps. Her words were hibernating
too, and like the bears, would wake. She let them sleep.

Changes

I know that they will fly away
in autumn skies, those feathered
choristers, leaving emptiness
perched on naked boughs.

I feel wings beating
in my bones.

As the leaves fall, in treetops
stragglers search for food
to fatten for the long flight,
their wordless tunes un-tuned.

I am putting away my summer,
storing it in boxes.

They depart in a chill night sky
searching for southern warmth,
winged shadows across the moon's
bright lantern.

Tenacity

after Charles Burchfield, "The Constant Leaf"

On soil cold as hearts that do not beat,
snow falls where trees are thin and bare.
Now flesh on old bones shivers with defeat,
no warmth and no relief from dark despair.
And yet a single oak leaf, dry and brown,
remains and waits for spring atop the snow,
its brittle points thrust upward from the ground
as if to fly aloft once more and grow
on limbs above that reach for summer's light,
where it will spread and open to the sun
away from shorter days and longer nights
an optimist although its life is done.
So we ourselves, our journey near complete,
avoid the earth that waits beneath our feet.

Backwards

I am riding south
on rails of steel,
back to the view,
eyes focusing on
what they've passed.
I feel like one of Dante's
soothsayers – body
condemned to walk
eternally in one direction,
head facing in the other,
punished for predicting
what would come.
When I was young,
I looked to the future –
there was only one
direction to go.
Now my past is much longer
than my future
and looking backwards
is a gift I'm happy to possess.
Going forward, or backwards,
sooner or later
we all reach the end.

I Will Cultivate My Garden

I will let go that cold in my bones,
rib-cracking, suffocating vise around
my chest, twisting tendrils of the old vines
that wrap my body tight. I will untie
the corset laces holding me in.
I will open to the dawns I have left,
the cool morning air, the phoebe's distant call,
robin's chirrup, chirrup in the elm,
house wren's rising falling trill, will rejoice
in my garden's rebirth, breathing in
the scent of hyacinths, daffodils, tulips,
rising rampant, new with bloom.

NOTES

Page 17: Guiseppe Fiorelli (1823-1896) was an Italian archaeologist working at Pompeii who invented a process of pouring liquid plaster into the cavities left by bodies enveloped by ash during the eruption of Mt. Vesuvius in 79 A.D.

Page 18: The phrase "so much gardening in the dark" is from Laura Kasischke's *Gardening in the Dark,* p 12; and "everything interesting including ourselves results from flaws or breaks in the symmetry" is from *The New York Times*, July 5, 2012, p. A1.

Page 29: Zhuangzi was a 4th Century B.C.E. Chinese Philosopher.

Page 66: "Proustian madeleines" is from Marcel Proust's *Remembrance of Things Past,* Volume One of *Swan's Way*. When dipped in a cup of tea, a madeleine (small pastry) evokes in the narrator a rich series of memories.

ABOUT THE AUTHOR

Phyllis Beck Katz's poems have appeared in many journals including *The Connecticut River Review, The New England Anthology, Ekphrasis, Bloodroot Literary Magazine* and *The Salon* and in two anthologies: *The Breath of Parted Lip: Voices from the Robert Frost Place* and *Birchsong: Poetry Centered in Vermont.* She is co-author with Charbra Adams Jestin of *Ovid: Amores, Metamorphoses—Selections,* and co-translator of M. Cecilia Gaposchkin's *Blessed Louis, the Most Glorious of Kings: Texts Relating to the Cult of Saint Louis of France.* She received her B.A. in English from Wellesley College, her M.A. in Greek from UCLA, and her PhD in Classics from Columbia University. She has taught English and Classics at the University of Illinois, Chicago Circle, City University of New York, SUNY Purchase, the College of New Rochelle, and Miss Porter's School. Since 1993 she has taught at Dartmouth College, offering undergraduate classes in the Classics Department and in the Women's and Gender Studies Program. She has also taught classes in poetry, cultural studies, and gender issues as part of the Master of Arts in Liberal Studies Program at Dartmouth. She and her husband, Arnold, have four children and eight grandchildren. She has traveled extensively and enjoys cooking, biking, hiking, and bird-watching.

This book is set in Garamond Premier Pro, which had its genesis in 1988 when type-designer Robert Slimbach visited the Plantin-Moretus Museum in Antwerp, Belgium, to study its collection of Claude Garamond's metal punches and typefaces. During the mid-fifteen hundreds, Garamond—a Parisian punch-cutter—produced a refined array of book types that combined an unprecedented degree of balance and elegance, for centuries standing as the pinnacle of beauty and practicality in type-founding. Slimbach has created an entirely new interpretation based on Garamond's designs and on compatible italics cut by Robert Granjon, Garamond's contemporary.

To order additional copies of this book
or other Antrim House titles, contact the publisher at

Antrim House
21 Goodrich Rd., Simsbury, CT 06070
860.217.0023, AntrimHouse@comcast.net
or the house website (www.AntrimHouseBooks.com).

•

On the house website
in addition to information on books
you will find sample poems, upcoming events,
and a "seminar room" featuring supplemental biography,
notes, images, poems, reviews, and
writing suggestions.